Table of Contents

APPENDIX

CHAPTER I

Introduction

The subject of this study is the emergence of the white supremacist movement as a critical criminal justice concern. White supremacists have strengthened their political agenda partly because their recent upswing in criminality is providing the necessary funds. This chapter identifies the boundaries of the problem, narrows the scope of this research study, discusses the methodology and organization of this study, and provides definitions of terms essential for discussing this issue.

Statement of the Problem

The last twenty years have brought a resurgence of hate groups and their racially-motivated crimes believed to have been nearly eradicated by the civil rights movement of the 1960's. Ironically, the decade arguably responsible for liberating discrimination sparked the birth of a new right movement that has been growing for two decades. Organizations touting white supremacy comprise the extremist segment of the new right. Nestled among the white supremacy ideology are Nazis, fascists, and a newly-reactivated and destructive group, the ultra-fundamentalist Christians. Their choice in using criminal solutions is gaining support among its members and affiliated groups mainly because of perceived gains. This should alarm all sensible citizens and criminal justice organizations should plan to contend with the inevitability of a white supremacist incident.

The emerging criminal conduct of white supremacist groups is much more focused on immediate remedies to their perceived problems. White supremacists were often unorganized and clumsy in their criminality, however successful bank and armored car robberies, assassinations, and bombings in the 1980's must remove any doubt about their potential violence.

1. In Denver, Colorado, Jewish radio personality host Alan Berg was shot to death outside his home on June 18, 1984. The Order was responsible for this execution.

2. In Ukiah, California, a Brinks armored car was robbed of an estimated $3.6 million on July 19, 1984. The Order conducted this daylight robbery.

3. Near Mobile, Alabama, on March 21, 1981, Michael Donald, 19, was abducted apparently at random, beaten to death, and hung by rope from a tree.[1] Two Ku Klux Klan members were convicted in 1984. In 1987, $7 million was awarded to the mother in a civil suit against the Klan.

4. In Sacramento, California, in June 1987, Greg Withrow, founder of the White Student Union was crucified by fellow

---

[1] Marilyn Marshall, "Beulah Mae Donald: The Black Woman who Beat the Ku Klux Klan," Ebony, Mar. 1988: 148.

members of the White Aryan Resistance (WAR). The skinheads of WAR thought Withrow had begun dating a Jewish girl and thus had denounced his philosophy. Withrow is reportedly still active in the Aryan Youth Movement.

5. In North Dakota, Gordon Kahl murdered two federal marshals in February 1983. The marshals were attempting to rearrest Kahl for a parole violation. Kahl was a convicted tax-dodger and a member of both Posse Comitatus and the Christian Identity Movement. Kahl was killed in a shootout later that year, but he is a martyr to tax protestors.

6. The Aryan Brotherhood, one of California's four major prison gangs, is known to deal in amphetamines obtained from their affiliation with outlaw motorcycle gangs.[2] A former member recently testified that the Brotherhood has targeted a number of Folsom Prison correctional officers for execution.[3]

7. In Ogden, Utah, in 1986, FBI officers thwarted a conspiracy to bomb an IRS office and rob an armored car in nearby Nevada.[4]

8. In Seattle and Spokane, Washington, between 1983 and

---

[2] California Department of Justice, Organized Crime in California 1984, (Sacramento: State Printing Office, 1985), 50.

[3] Wayne Wilson, "Hit Plot on Staff at Folsom: Supremacists' Plan Outlined by Inmate," Sacramento Bee, 17 Mar. 1988: B1.

[4] Robert A. Wood, "Religion and the Radical Right: The Tie That Binds," TVI Report 8, no. 1 (1988): 21.

1984, The Order robbed several banks and armored cars netting over one-half million dollars.[5]

9. In Arkansas, a state highway patrolman was murdered by Richard Snell, a member of the Covenant, Sword & Arm of the Lord (CSA).[6]

This list of crimes shows the range of criminal involvement by white supremacists. Further information and more detailed accounts of criminal activity can be obtained from two sources; Klanwatch Intelligence Report published by the Southern Poverty Law Center and the Anti-Defamation League of B'nai B'rith. TVI Report, a journal for the criminal justice profession, is publishing noteworthy articles about these and other domestic extremists.

Purpose of this Study

The purpose of this study is to review and describe the white supremacist movement, including its groups and their supporters, and provide a greater understanding of the scope of the movement for criminal justice practitioners. The purpose will be achieved if the reader obtains a greater understanding of white supremacists and their criminal activities while recognizing the debilitating effects of

---

[5] Joseph M. Melnichak, "A Chronicle of Hate: A Brief History of the Radical Right in America," TVI Report 6, no. 4 (1987): 39.

[6] Melnichak, "A Chronicle of Hate," 39.

hate crimes on society.

To fully understand the white supremacists, one must begin by identifying the central issues of the radical right movement. Primarily, these issues can be classified within these categories: an ultra-fundamental religious doctrine, political conservatism, and racial supremacy. Systematically, these groups align and name themselves after the one category that most properly describes their orientation, however, these groups remain tied to each other by bonds disapproved by the greater society. For example, Posse Comitatus, a tax extremist group, remains white supremacist even though the issues of tax and race are unrelated. White Supremacists believe that taxes support the Zionist Occupied Government (ZOG) and the money goes to affirmative action programs. This sense of hate bonds these groups.

Limitations of this Study

This study has three limitations which must be identified and discussed. First, there is no formal reporting of racially-motivated crimes in the United States or elsewhere. This limiting factor does not detract from this study, however, a national reporting of these bias crimes would statistically enhance this study. Secondly, the label, "racist," is not likely to be applied unless hate violence motivation can be substantiated. Racial motivation is not affirmed simply because the criminal and the victim are from different races. Finally, radical groups remain virtually unknown unless they voluntarily report their own existence or get identified by their criminal conduct, as in the Bruder Schweigend Strike Force II. This group was formed to replace the imprisoned members of The Order and conduct operations separate from the parent organization, the Aryan Nations Church.

Methodology

Library research is the primary basis for my thesis on the emerging white supremacist movement. Most of the information concerning white supremacy issues comes from reviewing the indexes, periodicals, and bibliographies of the literature at the campus library at California State University, Sacramento.

Pat Clark, the Director of Klanwatch, a project sponsored by the Southern Poverty Law Center, provided me with a large quantity of information for this study. Other resources were available from the Anti-Defamation League of B'nai B'rith, the Center for Democratic Renewal, and the National Criminal Justice Reference Service. Ciaran O. Maolain's The Radical Right: A World Directory and Laird Wilcox's Guide to the American Right: Directory and Bibliography were invaluable.

Definition of Terms

The following terms are essential in the discussion of this study. Except where otherwise noted, all of these definitions were derived from their usage by authors of leading publications in this field. Any in-depth historical discussion of this issue requires an expanded glossary, and some publications carry a specific glossary for that very purpose.

1. Affirmative Action: An institutional program providing advantages to minorities to repair past discriminatory practices. This is a rallying point for right-wing groups who feel that this is reverse discrimination.

2. Anti-semitism: An extreme hatred against Jewish people.

3. Extremist: A person or group that advocates the most extreme measures, and takes an uncompromising position.

4. Fascist: A person or group that advocates the establishment of a dictatorship, as in a totalitarian regime, that severely suppresses the rights of citizens to maintain absolute control.

5. Nazi: A follower of Adolf Hitler. A person with anti-semitic and racist beliefs.

6. Neo-nazi: Commonly used as a reference to those persons who support nazism today.

7. Racism: "The idea that ones own race is superior."[7] Some right-wing moderates believe the term, racially-motivated, "can be used to put any (white) person on a continuum that leads only to Hitler."[8]

8. Radical: A person or group advocating revolutionary changes in our social and political systems.

9. Reverse Discrimination: Whereas discrimination occurs against minorities by the dominate group, like whites, reverse discrimination occurs against whites because the system is designed to protect minorities. The groups discussed in this thesis believe that a program like affirmative action fundamentally causes discrimination against whites.

10. Ultra-fundamentalist: An activist whose political beliefs are supported by their unique religious doctrine.[9] This doctrine has many beliefs like a literal interpretation of the Bible.

11. Vigilante: A member of a group that takes the law into its own hands and uses whatever means necessary, especially violence, to enforce its own standards of conduct.

---

[7] William V. Moore, Extremism in the United States: A Teaching Resource Focusing on Neo-Nazism (Washington, D.C.: National Education Association of the United States, 1983), 135.

[8] "The Hitler Continuum," National Review 39 (30 Jan. 1987): 20.

[9] David Bollier, Liberty & Justice For Some: Defending a Free Society from the Radical Right's Holy War on Democracy (Washington: People For the American Way, 1982), 3.

12. White Supremacy: The belief in the superiority of white people over people of color; the belief that whites have a right to subjugate people of other races. "In racist lexicon, Jews are never considered to be white people."[10]

Organization of Study

This thesis is organized into four parts. Chapter I, as already noted, discusses the problem, the purpose of this study, the limitations of this study, methodology, and definition of terms. Chapter II is a review of the literature and contains a brief history of the emergence of the right, a typology of groups, and laws effecting extremists. Chapter III is a description of white supremacist groups categorized by their primary orientation whether it be Nazi, white supremacy, or religious ultra-fundamentalist. Finally, Chapter IV discusses conclusions and recommendations with a discussion of emerging issues and areas of further study.

---

[10] Thomas Martinez and John Guinther, Brotherhood of Murder (New York: McGraw-Hill, 1988), 39.

Chapter II

Review of the Literature

Introduction

The purpose of this chapter is to review the literature and provide the background information necessary for a scholarly discussion of white supremacist organizations. A typology of organizations must be examined as a prerequisite to categorizing groups as white supremacist. Finally, the history of the movement and its major organizations provide convincing argument for the persistency of this as a continuing social problem.

Typology of Hate Groups

Most laymen would label white supremacists as extremists or radicals; however, there are a considerable number of moderate organizations on the American political scene with de facto supremacist doctrines. In The Radical Right: A World Directory, Ciaran O. Maolain identifies eight diverse groups among the radical right in the United States; the conservative new right, the fundamentalist right, the ultra-conservative and anti-communist pressure groups, the more active anti-communist groups, revisionist historians, the anti-semitic and conspiracy theory pressure groups, white supremacists, and white paramilitary survivalists.[1] Maolain freely uses "radical" as a descriptor for all right-wing organizations.

White supremacist groups are operating in political, religious, and criminal arenas with a level of frequency found in the Palestine Liberation Organization (PLO). Le Mars, Iowa, Chief of Police Joseph Melnichak frequently describes certain groups within the radical right as terrorists in his writings.[2] While it is important to classify some groups as terrorist in order to identify their dangerousness, it is essential to understand that there are a number of political and sociological factors at work. Many right-wing organizations are sympathetic to these fringe groups. What was radical politics in the 1930's is now popular political ideology.

Racist/Anti-Semitic Ideology

The unifying theme among all white supremacist groups is their racially-pure credo. The supreme power of whites over all other non-white races, including Jewish people, is a belief sometimes masked but often openly paraded by Klansmen

---

[1] Ciaran O. Maolain, The Radical Right: A World Directory (Burnt Mill, UK: Longman Group, 1987), 337-338.

[2] Joseph M. Melnichak, "A Chronicle of Hate: A Brief History of the Radical Right in America," TVI Journal 6, no. 4 (1986): 41.

or Nazis. More dangerously, these groups despise other races, and this hatred is manifested in their political and religious doctrines.

Supremacists believe the U.S. Government and the economy are controlled by a Jewish conspiracy, and some groups even make references to our Zionist Occupied Government (ZOG). At farm auctions in America's heartland, white supremacists attempt to persuade empathetic farmers that ZOG and Jewish bankers are responsible for their economic problems.[3] Supremacists have been creating racial disorder for four centuries, but their recent efforts capitalize upon incidents that appear to be racially-motivated, such as the incident in Howard Beach, New York, when Klansman David Duke arrived and claimed a white victory.[4] The presence of white supremacists during interracial conflicts suggests racism motivated the incident. This tactic was employed by white supremacist groups during the Bernard Goetz incident, as well as others.

Political Ideology

The political agenda of the right offers ideal support to the fringe organizations of the extremist white

---

[3] Joseph M. Melnichak, "Domestic Terrorism in America," TVI Journal 6, no. 1 (Summer 1985): 17.

[4] Joseph M. Melnichak, "Hatred Continues . . . White Supremacists Update," TVI Report 8, no. 1 (1988): 15-16.

supremacists. Underlying a political ideology in which a racial bias is often apparent, there are many rallying issues. They believe the United States Government is too large and ineffective and should be reduced. Much of their effort concentrates on states' rights (over federal rights) and tax-protest issues. They would abolish the welfare system. Issues such as the busing of school children and affirmative action programs are quickly criticized by white supremacist groups as reverse discrimination. These groups are unwavering anti-communists. There are commonalities in strict discipline and rigid morality, as well.

The white supremacists are extremely political. A prolific use of publications, pamphlets, and books to spread their ideology is noted. A complete listing of publications produced by these groups would be too extensive for this thesis; however, a systematic review of their writings has revealed a total of 326 journals and publications of white supremacy.[5] The availability of other information sources is immense. Pamphlets, flyers, video cassettes, audio

---

[5] Anti-Defamation League of B'nai B'rith, Hate Groups in America: A Record of Bigotry and Violence (New York: Anti-Defamation League of B'nai B'rith, 1988).; John Liberty, Journals of Dissent and Social Change, 6th ed. (California State University, Sacramento: The Library, 1986).; Ciaran O. Maolain, The Radical Right: A World Directory (Burnt Mill, UK: Longman Group, 1987).; The Right Wing Collection of the University of Iowa Libraries, 1918-1977 (Glen Rock: University Microfilm Corporation of America, 1978).; and Laird Wilcox, Guide to the American Right: Directory and Bibliography (Kansas City: Editorial Research Service, 1984).

cassettes, dial-a-telephone, and computerized networks of hate information are but a few of the available resources. These extremist publications are sent to prisons, schools, dormitories, libraries, and to other supremacists and hate groups around the world. Often, this material is distributed to communities experiencing interracial conflict, such as college campuses, at a time when hysteria and racism are rampant.

Theology

Religion has created the crusading haters of the radical right. Their ministers teach a theology of hatred of Jewish, blacks, and other religious denominations and ethnic peoples. No religion or race should exist except theirs. Issues such as teaching creationism as science, preventing sex education, banning textbooks, and allowing prayer in school are a part of the ultra-fundamentalist doctrine touted by its ministry. White supremacists believe in the power and importance of the family and strict moral discipline. Jewish people are perceived as the murderers of the one true God and the true seeds of Satan. The worshippers of this faith are as fanatical and willing to violate societal laws to support their cause as were any of the religious fanatics in earlier history. These ministers have created a Christian outreach program that targets white prisoners.

The Emergence of the White Supremacist Movement

The roots of white supremacy began in this country. In the 1600's, most colonists, white and Negro, arriving in the new world were indentured servants. By mid-century, freemen, like plantation owners, began regarding Negroes as servants for life, and they passed laws to that effect. Segregation laws were enacted to separate the working class whites from the Negroes, because, by this time, they had developed a common bond. Vigilantes united to destroy this bond. Later on medical, religious, and scientific information would be distorted to support supremacist doctrines.

The Ku Klux Klan

Civil War veterans in Pulaski, Tennessee, founded the KKK as a social organization in 1865. The KKK has been resurrected in force on three separate occasions in American history. Historians contend that the Klan's initial growth spurt was due in part to the social changes (mainly the fear of freed blacks) and reconstruction effort (mainly northerners referred to as carpetbaggers) required after the civil war. The Klan terrorized the South committing thousands of lynchings, shootings, whipping, tortures, and mutilations.[6] Public pressure from above the Mason-Dixon line drove Congress to thoroughly investigate the Klan's activities and enact legislation to dissolve the Klan. As quickly as it had begun, the KKK disappeared for the next four decades. Many people feared the KKK still flourished as an invisible empire, however very little evidence substantiates this myth.

In 1915, William Simmons formed the new Klan in Atlanta, Georgia. Growing anti-Catholic, anti-Black, and anti-Semitic attitudes in America were common. Bigotry was at its height. In 1920, Simmons hired two publicity agents and the Klan began its expansion. Soon it was a big business named The Invisible Empire, Knights of the Ku Klux Klan. The Klan were the moral police, and soon their list of enemies included "Asians, immigrants, bootleggers, dope, graft, night-clubs and road houses, violation of the Sabbath, sex, pre- and extra-marital escapades and scandalous behavior."[7] During this period immediately following the "war to end all wars," the Klan's success in obtaining political power helped them amass a membership over 4 million strong and this time the Klan was truly a

---

[6] Anti-Defamation League of B'nai B'rith, Hate Groups in America: A Record of Bigotry and Violence (New York: Anti-Defamation League of B'nai B'rith, 1988), 75.

[7] John Turner and et al., The Ku Klux Klan: A History of Racism and Violence, 2nd ed. (Montgomery: Klanwatch, 1986), 16.

national organization. As America's economy stabilized and fears subsided, the power of the Klan began to fade, again. Their demise was hastened by internal power struggles over their acquired wealth and poor publicity resulting from their violence as well as a series of scandals.

The third Klan began forming after World War II in Atlanta, Georgia, but didn't begin to flourish until after the 1954 Supreme Court Decision on school desegregation; Brown v. Board of Education of Topeka. Civil rights issues throughout the next two decades fueled the fire of hate groups. The contemporary Klan is, in fact, a number of separate organizations with independent leadership, but their affiliation provides a strong form of unification.

Further information on the history of the Ku Klux Klan can be found in The Invisible Empire by William Katz, Hooded Americanism by David Chambers, and Hate Groups in America by the Anti-Defamation League of B'nai B'rith. Two other publications, The Ku Klux Klan: A History of Racism and Violence by John Turner and et al., available from Klanwatch, and Violence, The Ku Klux Klan and the Struggle for Equality by the Connecticut Education Association, are concise and available from the Center for Democratic Renewal.

Nazi and Neo-Nazi

The origins of Nazism and the atrocities of Adolph Hitler are taught to all American children as a lesson in hate which should never be forgotten. The substance of the Nazi movement has not changed since its origin. Nazism has long been viewed as the imported version of white supremacy and racism, but some sociological studies indicate that Nazism's roots came from a Marxist view of Charles Darwin's Origin of the Species. Nazi ideology in the United States can be traced to 1933 when Heinz Spanknoebel founded the short-lived Friends of the New Germany. The German-American Bund succeeded the Friends, but disbanded in 1941 when the U.S. declared war on the Axis Powers.

Neo-Nazism is attributed to George Lincoln Rockwell's American Nazi Party, founded in 1958 in Arlington, Virginia. Some organizations with Nazi doctrine concealed themselves as socialists, but Rockwell's success began because he was the first to openly espouse Nazism in post-World War II. After his death in 1967, Rockwell's party de-emphasized their affiliation with Nazism and its symbols. Consequently, the organization splintered into several smaller groups where it continues today.

The new philosophy of these neo-Nazi groups has been to minimize or deny any linkage to Hitler, swastikas, or violence. They have affiliated with the Aryan Nations and other white supremacist organizations for support. Many anti-semitic publications have been written, and recent writings claiming that the Jewish Holocaust never occurred have gained support in the world of extremists.

Further information on Nazis and the neo-Nazi movement can be found in these publications by the Anti-Defamation League of B'nai B'rith; Hate Groups in America: A Record of Bigotry and Violence, 1988, and Extremism on the Right, 1983. Teachers may find William V. Moore's book, Extremism in the United States: A Teaching Resource Focusing on Neo-Nazism, 1983, to be useful as a curriculum guide.

The Identity Church

> Religion constitutes a world and makes that world hang together. Through its rituals and symbols, religion shapes the attitudes of the people, tells them what the world really is like down deep, and what one can expect of life itself. One can never really know the group until one knows its religion.[8]

Perhaps the most threatening of all hate groups, the Identity Church uses the teachings of Jesus Christ to create Christian crusaders for the cause of white supremacy. This philosophy, called Anglo-Israelism, was founded around 1871 in Great Britain and came to America during the late-19th Century. This doctrine explains that Anglo-Saxons are the lost tribes of Israel, and are therefore the Chosen People. This religion may have been dormant until the mid-20th

---

[8] John Helgeland, "The Religion of Terrorism and the Mind of Gordon Kahl," TVI Report 8, no. 1 (1988): 23.

century.

The late Wesley Swift is credited with resurrecting the doctrine in 1946 when he established the Church of Jesus Christ Christian in California. Swift contended that Jews are the sons of Cain, who was born from Satan and Eve.[9] Richard Butler has continued the movement by moving the Church to Hayden Lake, Idaho, where he created an Aryan Nations. There are Identity Churches in almost every state, and the church has a prison outreach program to recruit white prisoners.

Further information on the Identity Church can be found in these publications of the Anti-Defamation League of B'nai B'rith: "The 'Identity Churches': A Theology of Hate," ADL Facts, 1983, Extremism on the Right, 1983, and Hate Groups in America: A Record of Bigotry and Violence, 1988. Joseph M. Melnichak has written several noteworthy articles for TVI Report: "A Chronicle of Hate: A Brief History of the Radical Right in America," "Domestic Terrorism in America," and "Hatred Continues ... White Supremacists Update." James Coates book, Armed and Dangerous: The Rise of the Survivalist Right, 1987, discusses the movement from the survivalist perspective.

---

[9] Thomas Martinez and John Guinther, Brotherhood of Murder, (New York: McGraw-Hill, 1988), 28.

Chapter III

Hate Groups

Introduction

The emergence of hate groups is a phenomenon of activity unknown to most Americans. The following alphabetical listing of hate groups, and their supporting organizations, reveals the complex dimensions of this violent subculture. These groups comprise only a small segment of the United States population and it is extremely difficult to identify the interwoven network of hate created by these organizations. More information is obtainable from the Anti-Defamation League of B'nai B'rith, Laird Wilcox's Guide to the American Right: Directory and Bibliography, or from Ciaran O. Maolain's The Radical Right: A World Directory.[1]

Hate Groups

Action Society: San Francisco

Orientation: Fascist
History: Active in mid-1980s, this organization follows the policies and philosophies of Oswald Mosley, the late British fascist leader.

America First Committee: Chicago

---

[1] Anti-Defamation League of B'nai B'rith, 823 United Nations Plaza, New York, NY 10017; Ciaran O. Maolain, The Radical Right: A World Directory (Burnt Mill, UK: Longman Group, 1987): 336-416.; and Laird M. Wilcox, Guide to the American Right: Directory and Bibliography (Kansas City: Editorial Research Service, 1984).

Orientation: Neo-Nazi
History: The Committee became active after separating from the American Nazi Party in 1985.
Policies: This organization believes in uniting white and black supremacist groups, like the Nation of Islam, to establish separate homelands.

American Covenant Church: Medford, Oregon

Orientation: Identity Church
Publications: American Covenant Newsletter

American Immigration Control Foundation (AICF): Monterey, VA

Orientation: Anti-immigration
History: An organization active in the early 1980s.
Policy: Their white supremacist orientation is concealed.
Membership: In 1985, they claimed 80,000
Publications: Border Watch, six per year.

American Independent Party (AIP): Lemon Grove, CA

Orientation: Right-wing Populist
History: An organization founded to support the presidential bid of George C. Wallace, the former Governor of Alabama, and early racist. His perceived reputation is the reason for the organization's continued listing among these groups.
Policy: This organization is anti-communist, and opposes gun control, income tax, abortion, and immigration. This organization supports a strong national defense, free enterprise, and individual liberty.
Membership: 170,000 (Primarily in California and Georgia).
Publications: Statesman Newsletter, monthly.

American Knights: California

Orientation: Ku Klux Klan
History: This is one of the ten small factions of KKK that are not aligned with national KKK leadership. There are less than 500 members among the ten factions.

American National Socialist Party (ANSP): Claremont, CA

<u>Orientation</u>: Nazi
<u>History</u>: This organization began in Anaheim, California, as a branch of the American Nazi Party.
<u>Publications</u>: <u>New Facts</u>.

American Nazi Party (ANP): Chicago, but originally El Monte, CA

<u>Orientation</u>: Nazi
<u>History</u>: In 1970, this group was formed by Frank Collin, an expelled member of the National Socialist White People's Party (now the New Order). Their original name was the National Socialist Party of America (NSPA), which is still used on occasion. Collin was expelled from NSWPP after he was identified as part Jewish, and he has been convicted of child abuse. Harold Covington (see Excalibur) led the group for a short time.

Some members of this group were involved in the attempted klan invasion of the Caribbean island of Dominica and other criminal conspiracies. In 1978, the ANP gained national notoriety when they attempted to march through Skokie, IL, a prominently Jewish suburb. In an effort to bar the march, the city legislators passed several ordinances which the US Supreme Court later ruled unconstitutional.

The media often incorrectly identifies all national socialist groups as members of this Party. This group is only remotely related to the original ANP founded by George Lincoln Rockwell (see New Order).
<u>Policy</u>: They are white supremacist and anti-semitic.

American Revolutionary Army (ARA): Atlanta, GA

<u>Orientation</u>: Neo-Nazi
<u>History</u>: The Army was active during the last decade.
<u>Policy</u>: They advocated revolutionary violence to overthrow the Government.

American White Nationalist Party (AWNP): Columbus, OH

<u>Orientation</u>: Neo-Nazi
<u>History</u>: An organization founded by the Gerhardt brothers about 1973 and possibly a member of the White Confederacy Alliance. The brothers were incarcerated from 1979 until 1983 on conspiracy charges to bomb an elementary school to protest a court-ordered busing plan.
<u>Policy</u>: They are white supremacist and anti-semitic and such national socialist policies as a revisionist history.
<u>Publications</u>: A bulletin, <u>White Unity</u> (originally <u>The White Nationalist</u>)

American Workers Party: Bartlesville, OK

<u>Orientation</u>: Neo-Nazi
<u>History</u>: Founded in 1975 by Clifford D. Herrington as the National Socialist Movement (NSM). Herrington frequently discusses his philosophy on radio talk shows.
<u>Policy</u>: White supremacist, anti-semitic, and revisionist historian.
<u>Publications</u>: <u>Social Justice</u>, every two weeks, <u>National Socialist Bulletin</u>, monthly, and <u>NS Nationaler</u>, six per year. An internal newsletter, <u>Brief</u>.

Arizona Patriots: Phoenix, AR

<u>Orientation</u>: Identity Church
<u>History</u>: Eight members of this organization were arrested on conspiracy charges in 1986. The group planned an armored car robbery, the bombing of a synagogue and an IRS facility, and they had detailed blueprints of three US dams.

Aryan Brotherhood: Nationwide

<u>Orientation</u>: Identity Church
<u>History</u>: This is the name taken by white gangs in many state prisons.

Aryan Nations: Hayden Lake, ID

<u>Orientation</u>: Identity Church, neo-Nazi
<u>History</u>: This organization was founded in the early 1970s by Rev. Richard Butler as a successor to Rev. Wesley Swift's identity church. Aryan Nations is the secular arm of the Church of Jesus Christ Christian. Two of the most violent supremacist organizations, The Order and Bruders Schweigen, were formed from Aryan Nations members.
<u>Policy</u>: They seek the establishment of a white nation in the Pacific Northwest.
<u>Publications</u>: <u>National Chronicle</u>, bi-monthly, <u>Aryan Nations Newsletter</u>, <u>The Way</u>, and <u>Calling Our Nation</u>.

Aryan People's Party: (See Social Nationalist Aryan People's Party)

Aryan Youth Movement: (See White Aryan Resistance and White Student Union)

Bandidos: (See Outlaw Motorcycle Gangs)

Brave America: Los Angeles, CA

Orientation: White supremacist, fascist
History: This is an information service on white supremacy and fascist groups in the US and was established in the 1980s.

Bruder Schweigen Strike Force II: See Aryan Nations

Orientation: Identity Church, neo-Nazi
History: A defunct criminal arm of Aryan Nations, this organization attempted a grand scale counterfeit operation and other crimes of violence. They were mostly unsuccessful.

Christian America Advocates: Mooreland, OK

Orientation: Identity Church
Publications: Christian America Advocates

Christian Conservative Churches of America: (See Christian Patriots Defense League)

Christian Defense League (CDL): Baton Rouge or Metairie, LA

Orientation: Identity Church, neo-Nazi
History: James K. Warner found and led this organization in the early 1980s as the extremist arm of his New Christian Crusade Church, an Identity Church. The name "CDL" ridicules the terrorist group, the Jewish Defense League (JDL).
Policy: Anti-semitic
Publications: CDL Report, monthly, World Economic Review, and Christian Vanguard.

Christian Identity Movement: Nationwide

Orientation: Identity Church, neo-Nazi
History: As described in Chapter II, this is the name applied to a group of ultra-fundamentalist Christian Churches that preach Anglo-Israelism.
Policy: Anti-semitic. They seek the establishment of an

all-white nation in the Pacific Northwest.
<u>Membership</u>: 6,000

Christian Knights of the Ku Klux Klan: North Carolina

<u>Orientation</u>: White supremacist
<u>History</u>: This organization recruits outside the state with limited success. They frequently march to publicize their policies and enhance recruitment.
<u>Policy</u>: Anti-semitic and neo-nazi
<u>Membership</u>: 200-500

Christian Patriots Defense League (CPDL): Flora, IL

<u>Orientation</u>: Identity Church, survivalist
<u>History</u>: An organization founded in 1959 by millionaire John R. Harrell as the Christian Conservative Churches of America. Harrell remains the CPDL leader.
<u>Policy</u>: Anti-semitic, para-military, survivalist
<u>Publications</u>: <u>Christian Patriot Crusader</u> and <u>Paul Revere Club</u>

Christian Vikings of America: Indianapolis, IN

<u>Orientation</u>: Neo-Nazi
<u>History</u>: This is a small branch of the National Socialist Movement's White Confederacy alliance active during the 1970s.
<u>Policy</u>: White-supremacist

Church of Israel: Schell City, Missouri

<u>Orientation</u>: Identity Church
<u>History</u>: The pastor of this Church is Dan Gayman.
<u>Publications</u>: <u>Watchman</u>

Church of Jesus Christ Christian: Hayden Lake, ID

<u>Orientation</u>: Identity Church, neo-Nazi
<u>History</u>: Founded and led by Rev. Richard Butler, a retired aeronautical engineer. This Church provides a Christian outreach program to many state prisons. Some Department of Corrections personnel have testified that Church literature is responsible for the creation of the Aryan Brotherhood (See Aryan Nations or Chapter II for more detail).
<u>Policy</u>: Anti-semitic and white supremacist. They seek

the creation of a white-only nation in the Pacific Northwest.
Publications: Some pamphlets and flyers.
Membership: Congregation of 10.

Church of the Creator: Otto, North Carolina

Orientation: Identity Church
Publications: Racial Loyalty

Citizens' Councils of America (CCA): Jackson, MS

Orientation: White supremacist
History: Founded in 1954 to counter the influence of the black civil rights movement, this organization is active in several states, includin., Alabama, Arkansas, California (4), Florida (2), Kentucky, Louisiana (2), Mississippi (9), South Carolina (4), Tennessee (3), and Texas (3).
Policy: The Council is pro-segregation, believing that states should maintain authority to determine racial policies.
Membership: The Council claims 750,000 in 1,000 local branches.
Publications: The Citizen, monthly, and The Spartan, which may have stopped publication.

Citizens' Council of America for Segregation (CCAS): Dallas, TX

Orientation: White supremacist
History: This organization is affiliated but apparently not controlled by the CCA and has been active since the 1960s. Originally called the National Association for the Advancement of White People, this group is not affiliated with the present NAAWP.
Policy: The Council is pro-segregation, believing that racial integration and marriages is a communist conspiracy to destroy America.
Membership: 1,000

Committee of the States: Mariposa, CA

Orientation: White supremacist and tax protest
History: Founded in 1984 by Identity Church leader retired Army Colonel William Potter Gale and others. Five members of this group were convicted in 1987 for threatening IRS agents and a Nevada State judge.
Policy: The Committee is a tax protest group.

Confederate Independent Order Knights: Maryland

Orientation: White supremacist

Confederation of Klans: Nationwide

Orientation: White supremacist
History: The Confederation is headed by Bob Scoggins and has been active, only recently, at the annual Klan rally at Stone Mountain, Georgia, in 1986.

Council for Social and Economic Studies (CSES): Washington, D.C.

Orientation: Fascist, White supremacist
History: Founded in 1980 by Dr. Roger Pearson as an ultra-right organization. Pearson has been an racist activist since he published Northern World in 1956.
Policy: Race and Eugenics
Publications: The Journal of Social, Political and Economic Studies

The Covenant, the Sword and the Arm of the Lord (CSA): Three Brothers, Arkansas

Orientation: Identity Church, neo-Nazi
History: Founded by former fundamentalist minister Jim Ellison in 1976. This organization is survivalistic and paramilitary. Criminal activities include the firebombing of an Indiana Synagogue, the burning of a church in Missouri, and the attempted sabotage of a major gas pipeline to Chicago. This organization concealed members of The Order from federal authorities. Federal agents were stunned by the camp's supply of weapons and explosives, 30 gallons of cyanide, and an automatic firearms manufacturing capability. Recent convictions may have disbanded the group.
Policy: White supremacist and revolutionary violence
Membership: 100 living in a secluded camp.
Publications: C.S.A. Journal. Several anti-semitic, racist and neo-Nazi publications are available for purchase from the official booklist.

Elohim City: Adair County, OK

Orientation: Identity Church

History: This City in an isolated area is a paramilitary group related in ideology to CSA.
Policy: Survivalistic
Membership: 35-40 living in the remote encampment

Eugenics Special Interest Group: Austin, TX

Orientation: White supremacist
History: Activated in the 1980s to provide scientific information to racist groups.
Policy: Racist. Promotes the concept of controlled breeding.
Publications: Eugenics Bulletin, quarterly.

Euro-American Alliance: Milwaukee, Wisconsin

Orientation: Neo-Nazi
History: Led by Major Donald V. Clerkin, its primary objective is to promulgate neo-nazi literature. The Alliance provides literature to prisoners and promotes prison pen pals among its membership.
Policy: Revisionist historian, racist, anti-semitic
Publications: Euro-American Quarterly, The Talon, monthly newsletter. Cassette tapes of speeches are also available.

Excalibur Society: Charleston Heights, South Carolina

Orientation: Nazi
History: Founded in 1982 by Harold Covington.
Policy: Nazi
Publications: Excalibur

Florida White Knights: Florida

Orientation: White supremacist, Ku Klux Klan
History: This is one of the few Klans unaffiliated to any national klan organization.

Forsyth County Defense League: Forsyth County, Georgia

Orientation: White supremacist, Ku Klux Klan

Georgia White Knights: Georgia

Orientation: KKK
History: The white prisoners in Georgia penal

institutions have formed the Georgia White Knights (also called the Georgia Realm).

German-American National Political Action Committee (GANPAC): Santa Monica, CA

Orientation: Neo-Nazi
History: Organized in 1982.
Policy: Anti-semitic and anti-gay.
Publications: GANPAC Brief, monthly.

Hell's Angels: (See Outlaw Motorcycle Gangs)

Heritage Library: Velma, OK

Orientation: Identity Church
History: Established in 1980 by Larry Humphreys as a residence and meeting area for Identity followers. Humphreys attempted to use this organization to forestall the foreclosure of farm properties. Humphreys is presently facing eviction because a bank foreclosured on his property.
Policy: Anti-semitic and anti-banking.

Identity Church Movement: (See Chapter II)

Independent Order Knights: Maryland

Orientation: KKK
History: This small group is unaffiliated with any other national or state klan.

Institute for Historical Review: Torrence, CA

Orientation: Anti-semitic, Revisionist History Group
History: Founded in 1970s by Willis Carto and Liberty Lobby. The intended objective of this Institute is to persuade others in to believing that the Nazi holocaust of Jewish people was a fraud. Their name and purpose are intended to lend credibility to their arguments.
Membership: Their mailing list has 30,000 names.
Publications: Journal of Historical Review, quarterly, Newsletter, and IHR Special Report.

Institute for the Study of Man Inc.: Washington, D.C.

Orientation: White supremacist
History: The Institute provides literature on race and eugenics and, like other groups of this nature, attempts to lend credibility to supremacist beliefs. Their circulation is primarily among fascists, Nazis, and other white supremacists.

Invisible Empire Knights: New Jersey

Orientation: Ku Klux Klan

Invisible Empire Knights of the Ku Klux Klan: South

Orientation: Ku Klux Klan
History: Founded in 1975 by an ambitious follower of David Duke (see Knights of the KKK). Bill Wilkinson formed this group in Denham Springs, LA, and later expanded throughout the South, Midwest, California, and Connecticut. This Klan considers itself a political party and sponsors a Klan Youth Corps (KYC). The national headquarters for this organization was in Five Points, Alabama, but may now be in Shelton, Connecticut, the home klavern of the present leader of this faction.
Membership: 1,500-2,000
Publications: The Klansman, monthly, and KYC News, quarterly.

Iowa Society for Educated Citizens: Iowa City

Orientation: Identity Church

Klan Youth Corps (KYC): Nationwide

Orientation: KKK
History: This was established by David Duke of the Knights of the KKK as a recruitment and training program for children. KYC activity is now present in many klan organizations and in several states and cities. Literature published by The White Student Union is proliferating this effort.

Knights of the Ku Klux Klan (KKKK): South

Orientation: Ku Klux Klan
History: Created in 1974 by neo-Nazi David Duke. This organization claims a lineal descent from the original KKK of 1865. Duke's use of radio and television talk shows for

publicity was successful in recruiting new members, but he was dethroned in 1980 and Don Black took the leadership position. In 1981, the KKKK conspired to overthrow Dominica, a Caribbean island, and Black was imprisoned for three years. The KKKK split into two separate factions, one in Tuscumbia, Alabama, and the other (Black's faction) apparently in Metairie, LA.

Membership: 500-750 in Tuscumbia, Alabama.
250 in Black's faction

Publications: The White Patriot, formerly called The Crusader. Both organizations publish The White Patriot.

Knights of the White Camellia of the Ku Klux Klan: Pasedena, Texas

Orientation: Ku Klux Klan
Membership: 40-50

La Porte Church of Christ: La Porte, Colorado

Orientation: Identity Church
Publications: Scriptures for America

League of Pace Amendment Advocates: Los Angeles, CA

Orientation: White supremacist
History: This organization is named after James O. Pace.
Policy: This group seeks repeal of the 14th Amendment to the US Constitution (States' Bill of Rights and guaranteed citizenship). Afterwards, the League would expel all non-white people.

Liberty Bell Publications: Reedy, West Virginia

Orientation: Nazi
History: George P. Dietz operates this company, the largest distributor of Nazi material in the United States. The company was originally named White Power Publications. Dietz was one of the first to establish a computerized bulletin board for hate propaganda.

Liberty Federation: See Moral Majority

Liberty Lobby: Washington, D.C.

Orientation: White supremacist and Anti-semitic.

History: Founded in 1957 by Willis Carto as a pressure group, Liberty Lobby is the central hub of a Carto's anti-semitic campaign. Carto founded the Populist Party, the Institute for Historical Review, and the Noontide Press and controls the National Alliance to further his anti-semitic aims.
Policy: Anti-semitic, anti-communist and anti-establishment.
Membership: In 1986, Lobby claimed 30,000 on their combined organization's membership.
Publications: The Spotlight and Zionist Watch.

Lord's Covenant Church: Phoenix, Arizona

Orientation: Identity Church
History: Sheldon Emry is the pastor of this church which, among other things, sponsors the "America's Promise" radio program.
Publications: America's Promise Newsletter

Ministry of Christ Church: Mariposa, CA

Orientation: Identity Church
History: The pastor of this Church is William Potter Gale, a retired Army Colonel, and one of the most prominent leaders of the Identity Church Movement.

Minutemen of Indiana: Danville, IN

Orientation: Neo-fascist
History: A relic from the national Minutemen network of the 1960s. The national Minutemen organization had attempted to infiltrate the army reserve and commence a violent political campaign against civil rights, communists, and a weak national defense. This group may be extinct.
Policy: The Danville group is white supremacist.

Moral Majority: Lynchburg, VA

Orientation: Christian fundamentalist
History: Moral Majority was founded by Rev. Jerry Falwell in 1979 as a pressure group for the beliefs of the ultra-fundamentalist Christian right. Their legal name has been changed to the Liberty Federation, although Moral Majority still sticks, and the Liberty Alliance is the designation for its lobby in Washington. Falwell also controls Liberty University. With a twelve million dollar 1986 budget, Moral Majority is formidable force in national politics. Falwell

has reportedly received this country's highest strategic briefing. In 1984, Falwell directed a voter registration drive to counter the gains in black and poor voter registration by Rev. Jesse Jackson. Falwell denied his motives were racist. In 1985, Falwell met with Bishop Desmond Tutu (the Martin Luther King, Jr., of South Africa and recipient of the Nobel Prize for Peace) and publicly denounced him as a "phoney."

Policy: The policies of this organization are the guiding morality for the entire ultra-fundamentalist Christian right. Anti-communist, anti-homosexual, anti-secular, and anti-feminist.

Membership: 4,000,000-6,500,000

Publications: Liberty Report, monthly.

Mountain Church of Jesus Christ the Saviour: Cohoctah, Michigan

Orientation: Identity Church

History: Founded in 1972 by Robert E. Miles, a Klansman convicted of bombing school buses in 1971 to oppose desegregation, the Church, sometimes called Mountain Kirk, has an active prison ministry and the religion is often called "dualism."

Publications: From the Mountain.

Nation of Islam: Chicago

Orientation: Black Muslim and Anti-semitic.

History: Under the leadership of Minister Louis Farrakhan, this organization has joined with white supremacists in expressing common views and objectives. Farrakhan has praised Adolph Hitler.

Policy: Anti-semitic and Black supremacist. Establish a separate all-black nation.

Publications: The Final Call

National Agricultural Press Association (NAPA):

Orientation: Neo-nazi, Identity Church

History: NAPA is alleged to be a front for the Aryan Nations. Beginning in the 1970's, NAPA was involved in farm loan disputes and unsuccessful lawsuits against banks.

Policy: Anti-semitic and pro-fascist

Membership: In 1985, NAPA claimed 3,000.

Publications: The Grass-Roots Courier, irregular, succeeds the Primrose and Cattleman's Gazette.

National Alliance: Washington, D.C.

Orientation: Neo-Nazi
History: Founded in 1970 in Springfield, Mass., as the National Youth Alliance and controlled by Willis Carto, the Alliance soon became a pawn of the American Nazi Party and leadership was given to William Pierce, author of The Turner Diaries, a Nazi guerrilla handbook.
Policy: Anti-semitic, promoting the establishment of an all-white nation in the Appalachian mountains.
Publications: National Vanguard, monthly, and Bulletin, monthly.

National Association for the Advancement of White People: New Orleans, LA

Orientation: White supremacist
History: Founded in 1979 by David Duke after being driven from his leadership of the KKKK. The name parodies the NAACP. The Association's goals were to organize racism among the more influencial and educated whites.
Policy: Anti-black policies, like civil rights, bussing ...
Membership: *2,800 in 10* branches
Publications: Action, monthly, NAAWP News, and other pamphlets.

National Democratic Front: Washington Grove, Maryland

Orientation: White supremacist
History: Formed by Garry Gallo in 1985, this organization absorbed the membership of the Southern National Front, formerly the White Patriot Party (WPP), which itself was formerly the Confederate Knights of the KKK. The WPP pursued violent means to achieve their goals. Some activities included arson, harassment, operating a paramilitary organization, and conspiring to bomb a restaurant.
Policy: The Front intends to be a political action organization and seeks an all-white nation.
Membership: 250-300.
Publications: The Nationalist and New America.

National Democratic Policy Committee: Washington, D.C.

Orientation: Conspiracy theorist
History: This is a Lyndon LaRouche organization once called the National Democratic Policy Committee in 1980.
Policy: Anti-communist and firmly committed to the idea

that there is a large scale conspiracy by Jews, communists, and others to overthrow the United States Government.

Membership: In 1984, the Party claimed 47,000. They have a constant staff of 200-300.

Publications: New Solidarity

National Determination Party: Manchester, New Hampshire

Orientation: Fascist

History: Founded in 1975 and originally called the American Majority Party until 1982. This organization advocates any policy to further the benefits to white Protestants.

Policy: Anti-communist. Pro-strong National Defense.

Publications: Imperative News and Views, monthly.

National Knights of the Ku Klux Klan: Stone Mountain, GA

Orientation: Ku Klux Klan

History: This organization splintered from the U.S. Klans in 1960 because they opposed its leader, Elden Edwards. This association firmly believes in the autonomy of the individual klaverns.

Membership: In the 1960s this was a strong organization of nearly 7,000, but today it's only one of ten splinter groups with a total membership under 500.

Publications: Imperial Nighthawk

National Legal Research Program for White Prisoners: Suring, Wisconsin

Orientation: Identity Church

History: This is considered the para-legal arm of the Christian Identity Church Movement and is supported by Aryan Nations and other Identity ministers.

National Socialist American Workers Party: Glendale, CA

Orientation: Neo-Nazi

National Socialist German Worker's Party - Overseas Organization: Lincoln, Nebraska mailing address

Orientation: Nazi

History: The NSDAP-AO was founded in West Germany by Gerhard Lauck in 1973, but later expelled.

Policy: They believe they are the successors to Hitler.

<u>Publications</u>: <u>NS Kampfruf</u>, a German quarterly, <u>New Order</u>, bi-monthly.

National Socialist League (NSL): Los Angeles, CA

<u>Orientation</u>: Gay Nazi and fascist.
<u>History</u>: The League was formed in 1975 and its use of the nazi culture may be attributed to sexual practices of sado-masochism.
<u>Policy</u>: Gay fascist

National Socialist Liberation Front: Metairie, LA

<u>Orientation</u>: Nazi
<u>History</u>: This organization originated in Panorama City, CA, in the 1970s. The Front is possibly linked to the American Workers Party/National Socialist Movement, the Identity Church, and other organizations. They operate an outreach program to recruit prisoners.
<u>Policy</u>: Nazi, fascist, revolutionary.
<u>Publications</u>: <u>Defiance</u>, <u>Siege!</u>

National Socialist Movement: Cincinnati, OH

<u>Orientation</u>: Nazi
<u>History</u>: This is a small but violent group of nazi activists developed in the 1970s. It may be related to the American Workers Party/National Socialist Movement in Oklahoma.
<u>Publications</u>: <u>NS Reporter</u>

National Socialist Movement: See American Workers Party

National Socialist Party of America: See American Nazi Party

National Socialist Vanguard: Goldendale, Washington

<u>Orientation</u>: Nazi
<u>History</u>: The group originated in Salinas, CA, then moved to The Dalles, Oregon, before its present residency.
<u>Policy</u>: They seek an all-neo-Nazi community.
<u>Publications</u>: <u>NSV Report</u>

National Sozialistische Deutsche Arbeiterpartei - Auslands

organisation (NSDAP-AO): (See National Socialist German Worker's Party - Overseas Organization)

National Socialist White America Party: Pacific Palisades, CA

National Socialist White People's Party (NSWPP): (See New Order)

National Socialist White Worker's Party (NSWWP): San Francisco

Orientation: Nazi
History: The NSWWP was formed in the mid-1970s from the NSWPP which is now the New Order.
Policy: The open promotion of Nazism.
Membership: Small.
Publications: The Stormer

National States Rights Party (NSRP): Marietta, GA

Orientation: White supremacist
History: This organization has been one of the leaders in anti-semitic hatred and fascism since its founding in 1958. Their most popular leader, J.B. Stoner received a substantial amount of votes in his bid for the Governorship and, later, for a United States Senate seat. The NSRP has long been affiliated with klan groups.
Policy: This group is noted for its desire to return complete power to the state. They believe states could then repeal civil rights legislation and establish white-only communities.
Membership: 1,500 (They have claimed 12,000).
Publications: The Thunderbolt, circulation 15,000

New Christian Crusade Church (NCCC): Metairie, LA

Orientation: Identity Church, neo-Nazi
History: Founded by James Warner in the mid-1970s. Warner also participates as a klan officer and is founder of the Christian Defense League.
Publications: Christian Vanguard, monthly

New Libertarian: Long Beach, CA

Orientation: Libertarian

History: This eminent libertarian journal advocates the denial of the Nazi holocaust. It is published five times each year.

New Nation U.S.A. (NNUSA): Morongo Valley, CA

Orientation: Identity Church
Publications: Citizen's Claw

New Order: Milwaukee, Wisconsin

Orientation: Nazi
History: This organization was the original American Nazi Party founded in 1959 by George Lincoln Rockwell. After his death, the name was changed to the National Socialist White People's Party, and after substantial debts in Arlington, VA, the group renamed and moved to its present locale. The group once used the name the National Socialist Party of America.
Membership: 200 members and 400 supporters. There are 40 local branches in eighteen states.
Publications: White Power, Dial-a-Nazi, and The National Socialist, the journal of the World Union of National Socialists is published by the New Order.

New Order Knights of the Ku Klux Klan: Overland, Missouri

History: This Klan has been supported by the National States Rights Party and is led by Rev. J.L. Betts.

New Order Legion: Portland, Oregon

Orientation: Nazi

The Noontide Press: See Liberty Lobby

Nordic League: Trenton, NJ

Orientation: Fascist
History: A Nazi merchandise outlet.

Ohio Knights: Ohio

Orientation: Ku Klux Klan

Order, Tne: (See Aryan Nations)

Oregon Militia: Oregon

Outlaw Motorcycle Gangs (OMG): Nationwide

<u>Orientation</u>: White supremacist

<u>History</u>: The origins of Outlaw Motorcycle Gangs can be traced to Southern Califonia in 1947. The Hell' Angels are the founding fathers of this movement which has spread across the world. OMG's comprise only 1% of the motorcyclists, yet their impact is substantial. Some sources estimate there are 522 OMG's in the United States.[2] The four most ominous gangs are the Hell's Angels, the Outlaws, the Pagans, and the Bandidos. These groups have chapters in 30 states. This establishes a network of criminality and a link between illegal narcotics, especially metamphetamines, and crimes of violence, such as arson, firearms, bombings, extortion, prostitution, and burglary.[3]

<u>Membership</u>: Outlaws: 25 chapters, 1200-1500 members; Hell's Angels: 33 chapters, 18 foreign chapters, 500-600 members; Pagans: 44 chapters, 700-900 members; Bandidos: 26 chapters, 500 members (There are 518 OMG's undiscussed in this brief).[4]

Outlaws: (See Outlaw Motorcycle Gangs)

Pagans: (See Outlaw Motorcycle Gangs)

Patriot Press: See Knights of the Ku Klux Klan

Pioneer Fund:

<u>Orientation</u>: Right-wing

<u>History</u>: Although this foundation was established to finance right-wing political research, much of its grants

---

[2] Phillip McGuire, "Outlaw Motorcycle Gangs: Organized Crime on Wheels," <u>The National Sheriff</u> 37, no. 2 (April-May 1986): 68.

[3] McGuire, 69.

[4] McGuire, 70-72.

went to Dr. Roger Pearson, a racist anthropologist (See Council for Social and Economic Studies).

Populist Party: Washington, D.C.

<u>Orientation</u>: Ultra-right populist
<u>History</u>: This party was created in 1984 by Willis Carto, the influential leader of Liberty Lobby and other anti-semitic groups.
<u>Policies</u>: The Party supports political candidates who are willing to fight the oppression of the middle class by the rich and the poor who are draining the budget.
<u>Publications</u>: The Party publishes a newspaper.

Posse Comitatus: Nationwide

<u>Orientation</u>: Libertarian right
<u>History</u>: This organization was founded in 1969 by Henry Beach, a life-long fascist. This extremist group is considered a terrorist organization. They are responsible for some of the worst violence among radical right groups. One of its leaders was Gordon Kahl, whose adventures were described in Chapter I. There is a strong tie between this group, the Identity Movement, and the Klan.
<u>Policies</u>: This group contends that authority above the county level is illegitimate, and its members refuse to pay federal and state income taxes. Farm foreclosures are considered part of the Jewish conspiracy. They are white supremacists.
<u>Membership</u>: The organization claims 2,000,000 members, but others estimate only 3,000.

Romantic Violence: Chicago, IL

<u>Orientation</u>: Nazi, Skinheads

Samizdat: Buffalo, NY

<u>History</u>: This is an anti-semitic publication originally from Canada. It advocates the Jewish Conspiracy Theory.

'76 Press: Seal Beach, CA

<u>Orientation</u>: Ultra-right
<u>History</u>: This company publishes anti-semitic literature and began in 1977. They are affiliated with many national socialist organizations.

Siegrunen Victory Runes: Glendale, Oregon

History: This is a Nazi publication that continues the memory of a particular German Nazi fighting unit, the Waffen-SS.

Skinheads: Various factions, nationwide

Orientation: Nazi, neo-Nazi
History: The Skinhead movement originated in England and then became linked to the neo-Nazis. This movement also resembles a youth cult. Rock music is a unifying theme; however, racism and nazism are not always a part of the group. Group nicknames vary like White American Skinheads (WASH), Chicago Area Skinheads (CASH), Bay Area Skinheads (BASH).
Membership: 20-25 groups in 12 states with 1,000-1,500 members.

Social Nationalist Aryan People's Party (SNAPP): Post Falls, ID

Orientation: Nazi
History: This organization was led by Keith Gilbert, who is serving a nine year term in the Idaho State Prison for welfare fraud and tax evasion. One other member of this party was arrested for killing two black men and another man mistaken as Jewish.

Soldier of Fortune (SoF):

Orientation: Right-wing mercenary organization
History: This organization provides a method of advertising for mercenary activities. Many of the national socialist organizations utilize SoF to facilitate their causes.
Publications: Soldier of Fortune, monthly, circa 200,000

Southern National Front: (See the National Democratic Front)

Southern National Party: Memphis, TN

Orientation: White Supremacist
History: This organization was affiliated with the White

Patriot Party's rally in 1986.
Policies: The restoration of white supremacy in the Confederacy.

Southern White Knights: Georgia

Orientation: KKK
History: This Klan is one of the independents. They separated from the National Knights of the KKK in 1985.
Membership: One of ten independent klans with a combined membership well under 500.

SS Action Group: Detroit, Michigan

Orientation: Nazi, Skinhead
History: This organization is led by young adults and is recruiting nationwide for members. They maintain a prison recruitment program, as well.
Membership: Branches have formed throughout Michigan and in Cincinnati, OH.
Publications: Michigan Briefing and Aryans Awake!.

Steppingstones Publications: Silver Springs, Maryland

Orientation: Fascist
History: This publishing company distributes white supremacist and anti-semitic literature. The White Legion, its original name, was established in 1973.

Stop Forced Busing (S.T.O.P.): South Boston, Massachusetts

Orientation: Ultra-conservative
History: This is a group that achieved notoriety in 1974 in their efforts to prevent forced bussing in the school system. Since then, they have attempted to campaign for the issues of the right, including stances against homosexuality, sex education in schools, gun control, pornography, and feminism.

Survivalist: Nationwide

History: The history of survivalist organizations is far too complex to be examined in this thesis. Many of the Identity Churchs are often called survivalist groups. The name implies a belief in the eventual nuclear holocaust of the world. Group members prepare to survive the ordeal by maintaining stockpiles of food, weapons, and civil defense shelters. These groups are often paramilitary and members are often affiliated with white supremacist groups.

Sword of Christ Ministries: Arkansas

Orientation: Identity Church
History: This organization has attempted to congregate prisoners into church sects.
Publication: Sword of Christ

Teutonia Film and Video: Hollywood, CA

Orientation: Nazi
History: This supply company features films and videos of national socialism and Nazi Germany.

Teutonic Unity: Buffalo, NY

History: This is a Nazi/fascist newsletter that began in 1980.

Torch: Bass, Arkansas

History: This is a fascist publication of the 1980s.

Truth Missions: Manhattan Beach, CA

Orientation: Revisionist history group
History: This organization was established by Dave McCalden after leaving the Institute for Historical Review in the 1980s.
Membership: Their membership may be the same as the Institute for Historical Review.
Publications: David McCalden Newsletter

United Klans of America (UKA): Tuscaloosa, Alabama

Orientation: KKK
History: This organization has retained a policy of low visibility. It is concentrated in these states: Alabama, Florida, South Carolina, North Carolina, Kentucky, Virginia, and Indiana. Their organization was devastated by the $7 million judgement directed against them for executing Michael Donald (see Chapter I).
Membership: 1,500. This organization has had as many as 50,000 members since World War II. As recently as 1967,

membership was 44,000.
Publications: The Fiery Cross

United Patriotic Front (UPF): Bartlesville, OK

Orientation: Nazi
History: This organization was established by the National Socialist Movement of Bartlesville in the 1980s as a successor to the White Confederacy alliance.
Policies: The UPF wishes to coordinate Klan and Nazi activities.

Western Guard Party: Buffalo, New York

Orientation: Fascist
History: This organization is a branch of the Canadian Party which seeks to continue white supremacist policies in government legislation. The Buffalo branch is primarily used to distribute their literature.
Policies: White supremacist and revolutionary policies.
Publications: Aryan

White American Bastion: (See Aryan Nations)

White American Political Association: (See White Aryan Resistance)

White Aryan Resistance (WAR): Fallbrook, CA

Orientation: White Supremacist
History: Tom Metzger, former leader of the California Klan, established this organization in 1980 as the White American Political Association, renamed WAR in 1985. WAR is affiliated with the Aryan Nations, the National Socialist Liberation Front, and covertly, the IEKKKK.
Membership: 5,000 members in twenty chapters.
Publications: WAR (succeeds WAPA Fact Ledger), Metzger hosts Race and Reason, a cable TV talk show.

White Confederacy: (See American Workers' Party/National Socialist Movement)

White Knights of the Ku Klux Klan: Queens, NY

Orientation: KKK

White Knights of Liberty: North Carolina

Orientation: KKK

White Patriot Party (WPP): (See the National Democratic Front)

White Solidarity Movement: Washington, D.C.

Orientation: Nazi
History: This organization was established in 1978.

White Student Union: Sacramento, CA

Orientation: Neo-Nazi
History: This organization was established by Tom Metzger of WAR as a youth movement. The leader of the group, Greg Withrow, was discussed in Chapter I as a victim of his own group. They crucified him. He survived and regained his leadership role.

White Unity Party: Pennsylvania

Orientation: KKK

World Service: San Diego, CA

Orientation: Neo-Nazi
Publications: Race & Nation

World Union of National Socialists: (see New Order)

WUN Enterprises: Greensboro, North Carolina

Orientation: Nazi
History: This company, founded in 1980s, distributes nazi and white supremacist books and merchandise.

Extinct Hate Groups

American Birthright Committee

American Christian Party

American Flag Committee

American Nazi Party

American Renaissance Party

American White Nationalist Party

Americans for Western Unity

Anglo-Saxon Christian Crusade, Inc.

Aryan Knights of the Ku Klux Klan

Christian Educational Association

Christian Party

Church of the Creator

The Columbians

Confederate Knights of the Ku Klux Klan

Friends of Rhodesian Independence

German-American Bund

The Herald of Freedom

The Order

The Plain Speaker

Right

Silent Brotherhood

Sovereignty Commission

United White People's Party

Other Hate Groups

Many recently active hate groups have provided little or no information about their organizations. Some may no longer be in existence. No investigation can identify all the hate groups. Here is a list of such groups.

Adamic Knights of the Ku Klux Klan

AKON/USA

All-American Bible Churches

American Committee to Restore Lawful Government

American Defenders

American Eugenics Party

American Front

American Majority Party

American Veteran's League, alias NSPWR

Americana Books

Anglo Alliance

Anglo-Saxon Books

Anglo-Saxon Christian Patriot

Anglo-Saxon Federation of America

Angriff Press

Anti-Communist Conf. of Polish Freedom Fighters

Appalachian Forum

Aryan Church of Greater Des Moines

Aryan Publishing Co.

Assoc. for the Advancement of Ethnology and Eugenics, Inc.

Association of Covenant People

Bay Area National Socialist League

Bob Jones University

Blond Network

Bibliophile Legion Books

Boniface Press

Capitol Contacts

Christian Constitutional Educational League

Christian Biblical America

Christian Educational Association, Inc.

Christian Identity Missions

Christian Israelite

Christian Identity Missions

Christian Nationalist Crusade

Christians For Truth & Religious Freedoms

Christ's Identity Church

Crusaders for Christ

Committee for Truth in History

Deutches Reich

Dilys Publications

Emissary Publications

Examiner Books

Falangist Party of America

Farmers Liberation Army

Frankhauser Ministry

Fluoridation Education Society

German-American Citizens League

Giallerhorn Book Service

Heritage Quest Foundation

Historical Review Committee

Holy Brotherhood Church

Holy Southern Church

Howard Allen Enterprises

Human Conservation Movement

Independent Republican Association

Independent Research

Institute for American Research

Logos Press

The Lord's Work

Majority Citizens' League

Manichaean Society

Message of Old Publications

Narthex Press

Mother Tongue

National Christian Democratic Union

National Council Confederate States of America

National Front

National Guard Party

National Socialist Bookstore

Nat. Society for the Preservation of the White Race

National Spirit of 76 Tax Study Foundation

North American Alliance of White People

National Socialist Student Alliance

National Socialist White Power Movement

Nutmeg Forum

Omni Publications

Order of the Flaming Cross

Patriot Bookstore

Patriots in Action

Phoenix

Racial Purity Bible School

Remnant of Israel

Rights of White People

Sons of Liberty

Southern Louisiana Citizens Council

Sovereign Press

Steuben Society of America

Task Force Dragon

Truth in Money

Truth Missions

Truth Seeker

United American and Captive Nations

United Racist Front

United White Christian Majority

United White People's Party

Uriel Publications

Valhalla Sales

Vinland Enterprises

Western Federation of Dualism

Western Front

White American Freedom Fighters

White Bookstore

White Christian Coalition

White Citizens' Councils

White Equal Rights Party

White Legion Books

White Majority Lobby

White Oak

White Party of America

White People's Committee to Restore God's Law

White Power Movement

White Youth Alliance

Summary

The purpose of this chapter has been to identify the white supremacist hate groups in the United States. A brief history has been provided for 108 autonomous hate groups and 111 others have been identified by name. Twenty-one extinct groups were also listed. This is clearly raw data that can be processed in many ways. Those who argue that white supremacists pose no problem might espouse certain information from this Chapter. First, the total number of groups averages only four per state. Next, the membership of most groups is low and combined memberships between groups is also noted, therefore the average number of members per group is low.

Criminologists might identify these statistics in a different fashion. First, these groups have volunteered information about themselves, and membership numbers and other statistics could be exagerated or understated for logical reasons. There are no estimates on clandestine hate groups or groups that refuse to respond to queries. One could establish doubt about the validity of this survey as a complete list of the white supremacist groups. Secondly, directories of the radical right are hesitant to label groups as "racist." In Guide to the American Right, Laird Wilcox chose to label many of the above listed groups as "conservative anti-communist" rather than as "racial nationalist," because the former predominates over the latter in group policy issues.[5] The Anti-Defamation League of B'nai B'rith and Ciaran O. Maolain disagree on the orientation of many groups, as well.

This information identifies a cadre of dedicated white supremacists who have established careers around these beliefs. They establish corporations, churches, publishing houses, and associations with relative ease and avoid financial difficulties. They are not kooks; they are

---

[5] Laird Wilcox, Guide to the American Right: Directory and Bibliography (Kansas City: Editorial Research Service, 1984), 1-2.

believers.

Chapter IV

Conclusions and Recommendations

Emerging Issues

The two emerging issues of the white supremacist movement are the proliferation of radical right groups and the "Hate Group Statistics Act" and other hate violence legislation being discussed in state and federal governmental offices and legislative committees. The radical right is emerging as a political force and extremist groups are among the crowds of supporters. Meanwhile, anti-hate forces are attempting to persuade legislators to enact a method of accounting for hate crimes and violence and dealing with it on both state and federal levels before it gets out of control.

The Radical Right: Emerging Fascism

A brief investigation of the current issues on today's political agendas should alarm any naturalized citizen who fled his or her homeland to obtain freedom of education, religion, and justice. Americans should always remember the tribulations of our early immigrants. The prevailing radical right attitude toward the rectification of criminal, moral, or political issues has been to espouse the establishment of tighter governmental controls. The issues have a certain commonality: the elimination of specific freedoms and inalienable rights on the pretense of giving the federal government more authority to protect its citizens, which is an argument more often used to promote fascism.

The strategy of the radical right must be addressed in this thesis because it supports, sometimes indirectly, the initiatives and beliefs of the hate groups. These issues are having a tremendous impact on legislators. The separation of the church and state has long been considered a founding doctrine within our government, yet radical conservatives are presently advocating mandatory religious prayer in schools, both tax credits and exemptions for private, parochial, and usually segregated schools, and the instruction of creationism as science in all public schools.[1] The Christian majority might profit from these policy changes; however, smaller religious sects and the secular population would be despondent. Religious freedom would, in reality, cease to exist and a mandatory religious monopoly might occur in our pluralistic and free society.

The education policy of the radical right would censor many textbooks and other instructional material, ban certain library books, teach creationism, abolish sex education, and

---

[1] David Bollier, Liberty & Justice For Some: Defending a free society from the Radical Right's holy war on democracy (Washington: People for the American Way, 1982), 43.

mandate school prayer.[2] Textbooks that teach the theory of evolution as well as literary classics from popular authors like Hemingway and Twain would be replaced by materials considered more ideologically correct by the radical movements. Educational freedoms are at risk if the ultra-fundamentalist party obtains a political majority.

More directly aligned with white supremacist ideology are ultra-fundamentalist policies opposing the equality of rights for women, children, and homosexuals, staunch hatred of communists, and the belief in the eventuality of a nuclear holocaust between the superpowers. Equality for some groups establishes racial, religious, and ethnic hatred for others. Until all humans are free from hatred, none can be free.

Effective Hate Group Legislation

Effective hate group legislation is a necessity for democracy. It must protect all people from violence committed by bigots. Some progress has been made in this area, but there are several critical issues to be resolved.

The 1961 Federal Racketeer Influenced and Corrupt Organizations (RICO) statute and subsequent amendments has been a legal edge for authorities cracking hate group organizations. Prior to the amendment and application of

---

[2] Bollier, 123.

RICO to hate groups, federal authorities had to rely entirely on violations of the Civil Rights Act of 1964 or interstate commerce violations of that act. In California, the 1959 amendment to the Unruh Civil Rights Act, other civil codes, such as the 1984 Ralph Civil Rights Act, and other penal codes and legal remedies have helped to curb the violence, intimidation, and discrimination of hate groups and other bigots.[3]

The Anti-Defamation League of B'nai B'rith has developed a prototype statute that restricts paramilitary training for purpose of promoting civil disorder.[4] Paramilitary training has been a commonly shared interest of Nazis, white supremacists, and survivalists. This statute has been instrumental in the prosecutions of several white supremacists.

The newest strategy in combating hate groups is legislation to collect data on crime motivated by racial, religious, sexual orientation, or ethnic hatred. Many states have adopted or are considering similar "Hate Crimes Statistics Acts." One resolution (H.R. 3193) has been supported by the United States House of Representatives and

---

[3] See California Department of Justice, Unlawful Discrimination: Your Rights and Remedies Civil Rights Handbook (Sacramento: State Printing Office, n.d.); and California Department of Justice Commission on Racial, Ethnic, Religious, and Minority Violence (Sacramento: State Printing Office, 1986).

[4] Hate Groups in America, 54.

the Senate is considering three similar bills (S.702, S.797, and S.2000). The bills differ only slightly, except that the inclusion of sexual orientation is questioned by some Senators.

Each of the bills suggests an aggressive undertaking by the United States Department of Justice, Bureau of Justice Statistics to collect data on the perceived motivation of criminals committing a variety of crimes. Some of these crimes are currently not reported in the *Uniform Crime Reports* of the Federal Bureau of Investigation, and some statisticians are concerned that law enforcement officials could not easily determine a criminal's motivation without the possibility of undermining the desired results either by guessing motivation or by compelling criminals to commit to motivation. Regardless of the support for this legislation by anti-hate group forces, the criminal justice system may not be able to achieve the goals promised by this legislation.

Some form of a Hate Crime Statistics Act is likely because supporters are suggesting a trial period of four years. All parties should be amenable to some resolution in this legislative area. This exploratory period should be studied carefully and the use of these statistics must be regulated to avoid desensitizing law enforcement personnel.

The Need for Further Study

Further research is necessary in two areas of hate groups research. First, the openness of many white supremacist organizations and the ease by which anti-hate group researchers gather information belies the anticipated and on-going actions of these targeted suspicious hate groups. There are some indications that this overt front of nonviolence may conceal a clandestine organization engaged in violent hate activity. The openness of these groups has placated the intelligence gatherers, law enforcers, and civil rights organizations. Secondly, recent racial violence on many college campuses has been obscured by the gangs of racists recruiting and looting in high schools. Many contemporary youth are choosing white supremacist lifestyles and are joining forces with the Nazis, the Ku Klux Klan, and other groups identified with violence and hate. These are issues requiring continuing analysis and research.

Clandestine Organizations of the Right

The term "invisible empire" has been associated with the Ku Klux Klan since the second coming of the Klan in 1915. This label indicated the organization's desire to convince non-klansmen that their influence was greater than speculated, and, essentially, the fear that this terminology instilled in people was successful in dominating an era of history during the 1920s. To some extent this "invisible empire" remains within the radical right-wing. While there are many average Americans who do not need or use scapegoats, it is possible that a few individuals may be susceptible to white supremacist ideology due to their imprecise information concerning those peoples of other ethnic, racial, or religious backgrounds.

The radical right, or new right, in recent literature has presented a persuasive political argument typified by hidden motives and agenda. White supremacists formed the first tax protest group and continue to be active in that movement; however, many prominent researchers and authors neglect to categorize them as white supremacists. Their policies remain anti-semitic. There are thousands of organizations with a radical right ideology. This may be the "invisible empire" described by the KKK.

Beyond the effectiveness of persuasive radical terminology, do "invisible empires" or clandestine organizations exist? The extent of clandestine hate organization operations within the United States is unknown; however, it is known that they do exist. A historical review of The Order is a chilling account of one such organization.

There has been no official government accounting of hate groups since the days of the House Un-American Affairs

Committee in the 1950's. The U.S. Department of Justice National Criminal Justice Reference Service could provide only three references on the white supremacist movement. The information on white supremacist groups is volunteered to researchers and journalists by the groups under investigation. Hate groups, which espouse communist and Jewish conspiracies to explain events, should not be envisioned as organizations willing to volunteer information on clandestine operations or to report illegal activities committed themselves or other clandestine organizations.

Youth Racism: Skinheads and the Klan Youth Corps

Youths are currently entering white supremacist movements at a considerably faster rate than have adults in recent decades. The skinhead movement, an form of racism exported from England, is growing at a significant rate. The Aryan Youth Movement, a recruiting concept developed by the White Aryan Resistance and White Student Union, is a California product sustaining substantial membership drives. The Klan Youth Corps may have been the first totally separate youth group. The emergence of these groups marks a significant decline in the beliefs of democratic equality among our contemporary youth.

Drug enforcement agents have discovered that juveniles and young adults pose a significant problem for the criminal justice system. Laws to arrest, convict, and punish drug pushers and control the crimes they are likely to commit are not applicable to juvenile court age offenders; thus, dealers have begun using youths to distribute narcotics and assassinate street competition. Many states have inadequate hate crime legislation and this seriously limits law enforcement in successfully controlling crime.

Summary

Emerging support for the rallying issues of the radical right and the enactment of legislation aimed specifically at hate crimes or groups are significant matters for public discussion and resolution. It is fortunate that the courts were willing to uphold the rights of individuals during debate in earlier years; however, certain political groups have recently utilized methods for impeaching judges who uphold often unpopular ideas. The endangered rights of individuals will require more support than can be provided by sensitive judges, the American Civil Liberties Union, and those anti-hate groups discussed in this thesis. Effective hate group legislation is needed in order to prevent the proliferation of racist, anti-semitic, and fascist motivated crimes supported by on-going organized Nazi, Ku Klux Klan, Christian Identity, and radical right syndicates.

There are no two criminal justice issues more devoid of

previous investigative study than those discussed in this thesis. The recruitment and acceptance of youth hate gangs has never been as significant in American history or as potentially dangerous to society as it is today. Is this the beginning of vigilantism expected from a dissatisfied society or merely a passing fad of an alienated youth culture? This phenomenon deserves intensive observation. Terrorism exists within the clandestine sub-organizations of America's known hate groups. Intelligence gathering agencies must continually investigate these organizations. Organized criminal activity and violent uprisings of hate group militants must be anticipated. Law enforcement agencies should continue to network intelligence gathering information.

Appendix A

Hate Groups By State

National Organizations

Aryan Brotherhood: Prison Gang
Confederation of Klans
Invisible Empire Knights of the KKK
Klan Youth Corps
Knights of the KKK
National Agricultural Press Association
Posse Comitatus
Skinheads
United Klans of America
Patriots: Tax Protest

Alabama

United Klans of America, Headquarters: Tuscaloosa
White Oak: Montgomery

Arkansas

The Covenant, the Sword and Arm of the Lord: Three Brothers
Sword of Christ Ministries
Christian Nationalist Crusade: Eureka Springs
Logos Press: Lamar
Message of Old Publications: Harrison
White People's Committee to Restore God's Laws: Bass
Christian Identity Church: Harrison
Society for Historical Research: Camden

Arizona

Arizona Patriots: Phoenix
Lord's Covenant Church: Phoenix
Kingdom of Yahweh: Sun City West

California

AKON/USA: San Francisco
Action Society: San Francisco
American Independent Party: Lemon Grove
American Knights
American National Socialist Party: Claremont
Aryan Youth Movement
Bay Area National Socialist League: San Francisco

California (cont.)

Brave America: Los Angeles
League of Pace Amendment Advocates: Los Angeles
Committee of the States: Mariposa
Ministry of Christ Church: Mariposa
German-American National Political Action Committee: Santa Monica
Institute for Historical Review: Torrence
National Socialist American Worker's Party: Glendale
National Socialist League: Los Angeles
National Socialist White America Party: Pacific Palisades
National Socialist White Worker's Party: San Francisco
New Nation U.S.A.: Morongo Valley
'76 Press: Seal Beach
Teutonia Film and Video: Hollywood
Truth Missions: Manhattan Beach
Truth Seeker: San Diego
White Aryan Resistance: Fallbrook
White Student Union: Sacramento
World Service: San Diego
Angriff Press: Los Angeles
Capitol Contacts: Malibu
Christ's Identity Church: Rough & Ready
Church of Jesus Christ Christian: Lancaster
Holy Southern Church: Van Nuys
National Front: Santa Ana
Omni Publications: Hawthorne
Western Front: Hollywood
White Hope Books: Santa Rosa
Holy Brotherhood Church: San Francisco
Informed Americans Assoc.: Santa Barbara
Ragew Press Service: Lafayette

Colorado

La Porte Church of Christ

Connecticut

Invisible Empire, Knights of the KKK
Anglo-Alliance: Greens Farms
Nutmeg Forum: Westville

Florida

Florida White Knights
Christian Educational Association, Inc.: Saint Petersburg
Giallerhorn Book Services: Crystal River
Howard Allen Enterprises: Cape Canaveral

Florida (cont.)

National Spirit of '76 Tax Study Foundation: Saint Petersburg

Georgia

American Revolutionary Army
Forsyth County Defense League
National Knights of the KKK: Stone Mountain
National States Rights Party: Marietta
Southern White Knights
Christian Identity Missions: Smyrna
Christians for Truth & Religious Freedoms: Snellville
Anglo-Saxon Christian Patriot: Snellville

Hawaii

Patriots in Action: Lawai, Kauai

Idaho

Aryan Nations: Hayden Lake
Church of Jesus Christ Christian: Hayden Lake
Social Nationalist Aryan People's Party: Post Falls

Illinois

America First Committee: Chicago
American Nazi Party: Chicago
Christian Patriots Defense League: Flora
Romantic Violence: Chicago
Dilys Publications: Chicago
Institute for American Research: Galesburg
The Lord's Work: Calumet City
Heirs of the Blessing: Herrin

Indiana

Christian Vikings of America: Indianapolis
Minutemen of Indiana: Danville

Iowa

Iowa Society for Educated Citizens
Aryan Church of Greater Des Moines
Remain Intact Organization: Larchwood

Kansas

Farmers Liberation Army: Halstead

Kentucky

Citizen's Council of America

Louisiana

Christian Defense League: Metairie
Deutches Reich: Shreveport
Invisible Empire Knights of the Ku Klux Klan (IEKKKK): Denham Springs
National Associaton for the Advancement of White People: New Orleans
National Socialist Liberation Front: Metairie
New Christian Crusade Church: Metairie
Sons of Liberty: Metairie
Southern Louisiana Citizens Council: Metairie
Valhalla Sales: Metairie

Maryland

Confederate Independent Order Knights
Independent Order Knights
National Democratic Front: Washington Grove
Steppingstones Publications: Silver Springs
Boniface Press: Takoma Park
White Christian Coalition: White Plains

Massachusetts

Stop Forced Busing: South Boston
Anti-Communist Conf. of Polish Freedom Fighters: Salem

Michigan

Mountain Church of Jesus Christ the Saviour
SS-Action Group: Detroit
Narthex Press: Dearborn Heights
White People's Party: Livonia

Minnesota

Falangist Party of America: Crystal Bay
The Instrumentality: Hopkins

Mississippi

Citizens' Councils of America (CCA): Jackson

Missouri

Church of Israel: Schell City
New Order Knights of the KKK: Overland
Missouri (cont.)

National Council, Confederate States of America: Maryville
White American Freedom Fighters: Overland

New Hampshire

National Determination Party: Manchester
Nutmeg Forum: Charlestown

New Jersey

Invisible Empire Knights
Nordic League: Trenton
Historical Review Committee: Rochelle Park
Task Force Dragon: Alloway

New Mexico

Suite Identity No. 220: Albuquerque

New York

Western Guard Party: Buffalo
White Knights of the KKK: Queens
Independent Republican Association: Glen Cove
Steuben Society of America: Ridgewood
White Citizens Initiative: Waverly
Yeoman Press: Cooperstown
W.R.S.P.E.: Bliss
Independent Research: Ithaca

North Carolina

Christian Knights of the Ku Klux Klan
Church of the Creator: Otto
White Knights of Liberty
WUN Enterprises: Greensboro
Crusaders for Christ: Winston-Salem

North Dakota

Uriel Publications

Ohio

American White Nationalist Party: Columbus
National Socialist Movement: Cincinnati
Ohio Knights
German-American Citizens League: Cincinnati
Truth in Money: Chagrin Falls

Ohio (cont.)

United American and Captive Nations: Akron
Blond Network: Dayton

Oklahoma

American Worker's Party: Bartlesville
Christian American Advocates: Mooreland
Elohim City
Heritage Library: Velma
United Patriotic Front: Bartlesville

Oregon

American Covenant Church: Medford
New Order Legion: Portland
Oregon Militia

Pennsylvania

White Unity Party
Appalachian Forum: Pittsburgh
Christian Biblical America: Morrisville
Frankhauser Ministry: Reading
Order of the Flaming Cross: Philadelphia
Western Foundation of Dualism: Reading
White Christian Church: Philadelphia
Manichaean Society: Reading

South Carolina

Excalibur Society: Charleston Heights
Heritage Quest Foundation: Simpsonville

Tennessee

Southern National Party: Memphis

Texas

Citizens' Council of America for Segregation: Dallas
Eugenics Special Interest Group: Austin
Knights of the White Camellia: Pasadena
American Committee to Restore Lawful Government: Arlington
Phoenix: Houston
A.K.I.A. Publications: Garland
Word of Christ Mission: Damon

Virginia

American Immigration Control Foundation: Monterey
Moral Majority: Lynchburg
Vinland Enterprises: Arlington

Washington

National Socialist Vanguard: Goldendale
All-American Bible Churches: Langley
Assoc. of The Covenant People: Ferndale
Remnant of Israel: Opportunity
Sovereign Press: Rochester

Washington, D.C.

Council for Social and Economic Studies
Institute for the Study of Man, Inc.
Liberty Lobby
National Alliance
National Democratic Policy Committee
Populist Party
White Solidarity Movement
Human Conservation Movement

West Virginia

Liberty Bell Publications: Reedy

Wisconsin

Euro-American Alliance: Milwaukee
National Legal Research Program for White Prisoners: Suring
New Order: Milwaukee
American Defenders: Milwaukee
Mother Tongue: Milwaukee

Bibliography

Abrams, Richard. "Free Love Ministries: An Army Under attack." Sacramento Bee, 20 Mar. 1988: B1-4.

Anti-Defamation League of B'nai B'rith. "The 'Identity Churches': A Theology of Hate." ADL Facts 28, no. 1 (Spring 1983).

Anti-Defamation League of B'nai B'rith. "Computerized Networks of Hate." ADL Fact Finding Report. n.d.

Anti-Defamation League of B'nai B'rith. "'Shaved for Battle'" Skinheads Target America's Youth." ADL Special Report. 1987.

Anti-Defamation League of B'nai B'rith. "The Skinheads-An Update on 'Shaved for Battle.'" ADL Fact Finding Report. 1988.

Anti-Defamation League of B'nai B'rith. Hate Groups in America: A Record of Bigotry and Violence. New York: Anti-Defamation League of B'nai B'rith, 1988.

Anti-Defamation League of B'nai B'rith. Extremism on the Right. New York: Anti-Defamation League of B'nai B'rith, 1983.

Anti-Defamation League of B'nai B'rith. 1986 Audit of Anti Semitic Incidents. New York: Anti-Defamation League of B'nai B'rith, n.d.

Audsley, David. "Posse Comitatus: An Extremist Tax Protest Group." TVI Journal 6, no. 1 (1985): 13-16.

Bennett, David H. The Party of Fear. Chapel Hill: Univ. of North Carolina Press, 1988.

Bogan, Christopher. "White Supremacy in Hayden Lake." Spokesman-Review, 19 Oct. 1980: D1-2.

Bollier, David. Liberty & Justice For Some: Defending a Free Society from the Radical Right's Holy War on Democracy. Washington: People for the American Way, 1982.

California Department of Justice. Unlawful Discrimination: Your Rights and Remedies Civil Rights Handbook. Sacramento: State Printing Office, n.d.

California Department of Justice. Organized Crime in California 1984. Sacramento: State Printing Office, 1985.

California Department of Justice. Commission on Racial, Ethnic, Religious, and Minority Violence. Sacramento: State Printing Office, 1986.

California Council on Criminal Justice. State Task Force on Youth Gang Violence. Sacramento: State Printing Office, 1986.

Chambers, David M. Hooded Americanism: The History of the Ku Klux Klan. New York: Franklin Watts, 1981.

Coates, James. Armed and Dangerous: The Rise of the Survivalist Right. New York: Hill and Wang, 1987.

Davis, Lenwood G. and Janet L. Sims-Wood. The Ku Klux Klan: A Bibliography. Westport: Greenwood Press, 1984.

Finch, Phillip. God, Guts, and Guns: A Close Look at the Radical Right. New York: Seaview/Putnam, 1983.

Fisher, William H. The Invisible Empire: A Bibliography of the Ku Klux Klan. Metuchen: Scarecrow Press, 1980.

Hackett, George and Pamela Abramson. "Skinheads on the Rampage: Terror Tactics by Neo-Nazi Youths in California." Newsweek, 7 Sep. 1987: 22.

Harley, Kathryn. "One Teacher's Prejudice." Maclean's, 27 Apr. 1987: 17.

Helgeland, John. "The Religion of Terrorism and the Mind of Gordon Kahl." TVI Report 8, no. 1 (1988): 23-26.

Jones, Clinton B. "The Criminal Justice/Racial Justice Nexus." Critical Issues in Criminal Justice. Eds. R. G. Iacovetta and Dae H. Chang. Durham: Carolina Academic Press, 1979.

Jordan, Pat. "The Aryan Mountain Kingdom: A Fantasyland of White Supremacy." Life, Nov. 1986: 22-26.

Katz, William Loren. The Invisible Empire: The Ku Klux Klan Impact on History. Washington: Open Hand Publishing, 1986.

"LA County Hate Crimes on Increase." Sacramento Bee, 19 Feb. 1988: B5.

Liberty, John. Journals of Dissent and Social Change. 6th ed. California State University, Sacramento: The Library, 1986.

Maolain, Ciaran O. The Radical Right: A World Directory. Burnt Mill, UK: Longman Group, 1987.

Marshall, Marilyn. "Beulah Mae Donald: The Black Woman Who Beat the Ku Klux Klan." Ebony, Mar. 1988: 148-153.

Martinez, Thomas and John Guinther. Brotherhood of Murder. New York: McGraw-Hill, 1988.

McGuire, Phillip. "Outlaw Motorcycle Gangs: Organized Crime on Wheels." National Sherriff 37, no. 2 (1986): 68-75.

Melnichak, Joseph M. "A Chronicle of Hate: A Brief History of the Radical Right in America." TVI Report 6, no. 4 (1987): 38-42.

---. "Domestic Terrorism in America." TVI Journal 6, no. 1 (1985): 17-19.

---. "Hatred Continues ... White Supremacists Update." TVI Report 8, no. 1 (1988): 15-17.

---. "Tactics of the Extreme Right in the Farm Crisis." TVI Journal 6, no. 3 (1986): 22-26.

Meyer, Eugene L. "Neo-Nazi Backer's Surprise." Sacramento Bee, 28 Apr. 1988: A25.

Moore, William V. Extremism in the United States: A Teaching Resource Focusing on Neo-Nazism. Washington, D.C.: National Education Association of the United States, 1983.

"1 Verdict in Supremacists' Trial; 2 to Go." Sacramento Bee, 7 Apr. 1988: A14.

Ostling, Richard N. "A Sinister Search for "Identity": Far-Right Groups Use Theology to Justify Violence and Racism." Time, 20 Oct. 1986: 74.

"Racists Force AT&T Minority-hiring Vote." Sacramento Bee, 20 Mar. 1988: A12.

The Right Wing Collection of the University of Iowa Libraries, 1918-1977. Glen Rock: University Microfilm Corporation of America, 1978.

Rossi, Peter H., ed. Ghetto Revolts. 2nd ed. New Brunswick: Transaction, 1973.

Seltzer, Rick and Grace M. Lopes. "The Ku Klux Klan:

Reasons for Support or Opposition Among White Respondents." Journal of Black Studies 17, no. 1 (1986): 91-109.

Sherwin, Mark. The Extremists. New York: St Martin's Press, 1963.

Simmons, Bill. "Jurors Acquit Racists: Supremacists Claim Victory." Sacramento Bee, 8 Apr. 1988: A21.

Skidmore, Gail and Theodore Jurgen Spahn. From Radical Left to Extreme Right. 3rd ed. Metuchen, NJ: Scarecrow Press, 1987.

Starr, Mark and George Raine. "Violence on the Right: A Handful of New Extremists Disturbs the Peace." Newsweek, 4 Mar. 1985: 23-26.

Suall, Irvin and David Lowe. "Special Report: The Hate Movement Today: A Chronicle of Violence and Disarray." Terrorism 10, no. 4 (1987): 345-364.

Talaga, Deborah Ann. "Historical-Analysis of the Ku Klux Klan 1865-1982." ths., California State Univ., Sacramento, 1982.

Turner, John and et al. The Ku Klux Klan: A History of Racism and Violence. 2nd ed. Montgomery: Klanwatch, 1986.

Vargas, Dale. "Woman's Suit: Ministry Kept Me Captive.'" Sacramento Bee, 16 Mar. 1988: B1-2.

"Verdict Delights Far Right." Sacramento Bee, 9 Apr. 1988: A16.

Violence, The Ku Klux Klan ar   Struggle for Equality. Connecticut: Connecticut Education Assoc., Council on Interracial Books for Children, and National Education Assoc., 1981.

Wade, Wyn Craig. The Fiery Cross: The Ku Klux Klan in America. New York: Simon and Schuster, 1987.

Weigel, Russel H., and Paul W. Howes. "Conceptions of Racial Prejudice: Symbolic Racism Reconsidered." Journal of Social Issues 41, no. 3 (1985): 117-138.

Wilcox, Laird M. Guide to the American Right: Directory and Bibliography. Kansas City: Editorial Research Service, 1984

Wilson, Wayne. "'Hit" Plot on Staff at Folsom." Sacramento Bee, 17 Mar. 1988: B1-3.

Wood, Robert A. "Religion and the Radical Right: The Tie that Binds." TVI Report 8, no. 1 (1988): 18-22.

---. "Gordon Kahl: The Legacy of an Extremist Hero." TVI Report 8, no. 1 (1988): 27-32.

www.ingramcontent.com/pod-product-compliance
Lightning Source LLC
Chambersburg PA
CBHW080520290526
45790CB00006B/2241
9781511760737